Collins *Little book of*

Crossword Secrets

HarperCollins Publishers
Westerhill Road
Bishopbriggs
Glasgow
G64 2QT

First edition 2011

Reprint 10 9 8 7 6 5 4 3 2 1 0

© HarperCollins Publishers
2011

ISBN 978-0-00-744316-1

Collins ® is a registered
trademark of HarperCollins
Publishers Limited

www.collinslanguage.com

A catalogue record for this
book is available from the
British Library

Typeset by Davidson
Publishing Solutions, Glasgow

Printed and bound at
Leo Paper Products Ltd

Contents

Contributors
Derrick Knight
Michael Kindred

Editor
Freddy Chick

For the Publisher
Lucy Cooper
Kerry Ferguson
Elaine Higgleton

Foreword

There have been other little books that have made far greater claims than this one. Equally, there have been many more that have sought only to spread the news of what the butler saw. This ***Little Book of Crossword Secrets*** lies somewhere in between. It does not contain a vision of a new global order and yet, in a world that has never been more puzzling, it does promise to answer some of the serious questions that keep you awake at night:

'Considering the end of days, confused in thy solo cage' (11) asking 'What lies quivering at the bottom of the deep?' (1,7,5)

The secrets divulged within these pages, along with lists of the most useful crossword words, will let you tackle crosswords with confidence and hopefully brighten up your day.

A BRIEF HISTORY OF CROSSWORD PUZZLES

The first crossword appeared in the New York Sunday newspaper *World* in 1913. A journalist, Arthur Wynne, had been asked to create a new game for the 'fun' section of the paper. Recalling acrostic puzzles from his childhood, he devised a diamond-shaped grid with clues for the words. He called this a 'Word Cross'. It later became known as a 'cross-word'. When the hyphen disappeared, the crossword had arrived.

The first British crossword was a 'quick' crossword, which appeared in 1923. A setter with the awe-inspiring pseudonym of Torquemada (Edward Powys Mathers) championed the cryptic element of crosswords from the mid-1920s. The first *Times* crossword was published in 1930; by then most British newspapers were carrying a crossword puzzle. A crossword-solving craze had begun which endures to this day, boosting daily sales of national newspapers and giving a focus to tea breaks across the land.

Cryptic and quick crosswords differ in that the surface meaning of a quick crossword clue corresponds to the solution, e.g. 'nimble' (5) has the solution AGILE. Quick crosswords tend to make use of synonyms (as above) or hyponyms, where the solution is a more specific type of the clue word; e.g. 'dress' (4) has the solution SARI. The challenge of quick crosswords is that the solver doesn't know whether their solution is the correct one: 'nimble' could be LIGHT; 'dress' could be TOGA. Solvers build up confidence in their solutions by using the checked letters of the unfolding grid.

The beauty of cryptic crosswords, on the other hand, is that solvers can immediately be certain that their solutions are correct. This is because there are always two ways to solve a cryptic clue. One aspect of a cryptic clue is the definition: a word or phrase which is a synonym or hypernym of the solution. The other aspect is the wordplay: a device such as an anagram, reversal, or charade which employs specific letters from the clue.

The clue as a whole is written so that the surface meaning distracts or actively misdirects the solver from the solution, e.g.

CLUE   *The flower of Glasgow?* (5)

The solver expects the solution to be a flower, not a flow-er, i.e. the river CLYDE.

Many crossword editors abide by the rules of clueing fairness set down by the pioneering *Observer* setter Ximenes (DS Macnutt). Ximenes wrote a treatise on the art of crossword clue setting, and is succeeded at *The Observer* in modern times by Azed (Jonathan Crowther) who has summed up his crossword philosophy as follows:

A good cryptic clue contains three elements:

- a precise definition
- a fair subsidiary indication (wordplay)
- nothing else

The opposing school of crossword clueing (non-Ximenean) is practised by Araucaria (John Graham), whose unique jigsaw puzzles in *The Guardian* have attracted a cult following for their ingenuity, wit, and occasional flouting of fair play.

Another 'cryptic' element of the crossword puzzle is the setter's pseudonym. Crossword setters have long concealed their identities with an allusive *nom de plume*. A good few refer to the Spanish Inquisition – Torquemada, Ximenes, Azed (Deza backwards) – but most make reference to the setter's real name or interests (e.g. some of Don Manley's pseudonyms are types of 'don' – Quixote, Giovanni, Pasquale).

CRACKING

CRYPTIC

CLUES

'Cryptic' means 'hidden', 'secret' or 'obscure'. Setters of cryptic crosswords are devious creatures who love to mislead solvers as much as possible, using phrases and sentences which appear to be straightforward English, but are in fact anything but! They are spies whose cover must be blown and their true identity revealed. They are emissaries of an alien world where everything is back to front and nothing is what it at first appears. Yet if this little book is to justify its name we must set about laying their secrets bare. So let's get cracking!

All good investigations into alien life forms begin with an autopsy and so will we. We'll start by pulling the clues apart and examining what they are made up of and the different forms and variations they can take.

The Bare Bones

At the most basic level there are only a few forms a cryptic clue can take. The first, and by far the most common is:

Definition Followed by the Wordplay

Example (with the definition in **bold**):

> **CLUE**   *Part of the body in the advert* (4)

Wordplay Followed by the Definition

Example (with the definition in **bold**):

> **CLUE**   *The advert includes **part of the body*** (4)
> **SOLUTION**   to **a** and **b**: HEAD

Explanation: The definition in both clues is 'part of the body'. In example (a) 'in' hints that the answer is hidden within the clue, and 'includes' does the same in example (b). 'Head', a part of the body, can be found within the words 'the advert',

The other types of clue are rarer. They are:

Double or Multiple Definition

Two or more definitions are put together to be
misleading. Each one taken separately is a definition
of the answer.

CLUE   *Scandinavian vegetable* (5)

SOLUTION SWEDE

Explanation: A Swede is a Scandinavian and a
swede is a type of vegetable.

Single Definition

The whole clue is a definition of the answer.
A question mark is sometimes used to emphasize
the misleading or humorous nature of this type of clue.
This example uses a very old joke.

CLUE   *What lies quivering at the bottom of the sea?*
         (1,7,5)

SOLUTION A NERVOUS WRECK

Definition = Word Play

In this kind of clue the definition and wordplay are not separated but instead lie on top of each other at different levels of meaning.

CLUE   *Part of regular curve* (3)

SOLUTION   ARC

Explanation: The definition is the whole clue 'part of regular curve'. 'Arc' is a part of a regular curve. 'Part of' also indicates that the answer is hidden inside the clue, as indeed it is: 'regul**ar c**urve'.

Working Out the Wordplay

It is the wordplay in cryptic clues that confounds most aspirant solvers. The trouble is that these wordplays are so highly evolved that they come in a bewildering variety. It is tricky enough to solve them when you know what kind of riddle they are and until you can work out at least that, you will struggle as fruitlessly as a man trying to pick bananas in a straitjacket.

We've categorised the weird and wonderful wordplays we've come across into 16 groups and find that they fit all but the most monstrous of clues.

The Simple Anagram

The letters of one or more words in the clue are rearranged to form the grid entry. An anagram indicator appears somewhere in the clue to let you know that some letters have to be rearranged.

 Danger: wild bird (6)

SOLUTION GANDER

Explanation: 'Wild' is an anagram indicator showing that the letters of 'danger' have to be rearranged. This gives 'gander', which fits the definition of 'bird'. The colon after 'danger' is intended to mislead the solver by separating the anagram indicator ('wild') and the word that has to be reordered to give the answer ('danger').

The Subtractive Anagram

In this type of anagram, the solver has to remove some letters from those to be rearranged to form the grid entry.

CLUE *Upset therapist disowned his disjointed glib talk* (6)

SOLUTION PATTER

15

Explanation: 'Upset' shows that this is an anagram of 'therapist'. 'Disowned his' shows that the letters H, I and S have to be removed from 'therapist' (and 'disjointed' shows that H, I and S do not appear together in the word). Once H, I and S have been deleted from 'therapist' the letters can be rearranged into a word that corresponds to the definition of 'glib talk': that is PATTER.

Most editors would consider it fairer if the letters that are to be removed from the word appear together in their correct order in the clue, for example:

> **CLUE** *Sharp blow taken from therapist upset sea nymph* (6)
>
> **SOLUTION** THETIS

Explanation: A 'rap' is a 'sharp blow'. If you remove the letters R, A and P from 'therapist' (indicated by the words 'taken from') and then rearrange the remaining letters (as shown by 'upset'), you get the word THETIS, who was a sea nymph in Greek mythology. The order of 'upset' and 'therapist' has been switched in order to produce a sensible sentence.

Split

The grid entry is made up of individual parts that are
put together in the order they occur.

> **CLUE** *Transport great weight in container* (6)
>
> **SOLUTION** CARTON

Explanation: 'Car' is a form of 'transport' and
'ton' is a 'great weight'. Combined they make
CARTON, which is a 'container'. 'In' is a linking
word included to improve the surface reading of
the clue.

Container and Contents

One component of the grid entry is expressed as being,
for example, 'in' or 'around' another component.

> **CLUE** *Attempt to include tree in ornamental decorative
> pattern* (7)
>
> **SOLUTION** TRACERY

Explanation: 'Try' means 'attempt' and 'acer' is
a kind of tree. Attempt is to 'include' tree, so 'acer'
has to be inserted into 'try', thereby producing
TRACERY, which is an 'ornamental decorative
pattern'.

Takeaway Container and Contents

In this case, part of a word is taken away to give the grid entry. (It might help you to imagine the word as a sandwich between its first and last letters, and some of the letters in the middle – the sandwich filling – are removed).

 Alan leaves substance plugging gap to harden (3)

SOLUTION SET

Explanation: The 'substance plugging gap' is 'sealant'. Removing 'Alan' from 'sealant', which is indicated by the use of 'leaves', gives the answer SET, which means 'to harden'.

Hidden Word

The letters that make up the grid entry are found in the correct order in one or more words in the clue. There must be no superfluous words in the clue.

CLUE *High temperature in the attic* (4)

SOLUTION HEAT

Explanation: Another word for 'high temperature' is HEAT, which can be found in the words '**the at**tic'.

Reverse Direction (either horizontal or vertical)

The grid entry appears in the clue, either back to front if it's in an across clue or from bottom to top if it's in a down clue.

 Anthropoid primate found back in the past (3)

SOLUTION APE

Explanation: The definition is 'anthropoid primate'. 'Found' indicates that the grid entry is a hidden word within the clue. 'Back' shows that it is a reverse direction clue. The words 'th**e pa**st' contain the letters E, P and A which, when written in reverse, give us APE.

Homophone (sound device)

A homophone is a word that sounds like another, for example 'bare' and 'bear'. The grid entry is usually another word for one of the elements in the clue, and is a homophone of the other element.

CLUE *One fruit or two by the sound of it* (4)

SOLUTION PEAR

Explanation: 'Pear' is 'one fruit' and 'pair' means 'two'. 'By the sound of it' shows that this is a homophone clue.

Deletion

Part of an indicated word is taken away, leaving the grid entry.

 Marionette gives up little dog to find tame animal (3)

SOLUTION PET

Explanation: A 'marionette' is another word for 'puppet'. A 'pup' is a young, or little, dog. Taking 'pup' away from 'puppet', as shown by the words 'gives up', leaves PET, which is a 'tame animal'

Moving Letter

One or more letters are moved to another position in a word.

CLUE *Many fit into a small space moving head to tail* (4)
NB: This has to be a down clue for 'head to tail' to be acceptable.

SOLUTION LOTS

Explanation: If 'fit into a small space' is 'slot', and you follow the instruction in the clue by moving its head (its first letter S) to its tail (the end of the word), you get the answer LOTS, which means 'many'.

Substituted Letter

One letter of a word in the clue takes the place of another.

> **CLUE** *Saunter, taking a different direction to get cash* (5)
>
> **SOLUTION** MONEY

Explanation: Another word for 'saunter' is 'mosey'. 'Taking a different direction' means changing one of the letters E (for east), S (for south), W (for west) or N (for north) for another one of E, S, W or N. (These direction abbreviations occur frequently in cryptic crosswords).

If you substitute the S in 'mosey' with N, you get MONEY, which is the same as 'cash'.

Odd or Even Letters

The grid entry is produced from alternate letters in part of the clue.

 Male creatures with bony appendages, even ones to be found in new lakes (4)

SOLUTION   ELKS

Explanation: The definition is 'male creatures with bony appendages'. The words 'even ones' show that you are to take every other letter, starting with the second one, from some part of the clue to produce the grid entry. You know to use the words 'new lakes' for this because the wordplay tells you that 'even ones' are 'to be found in new lakes'. Take the even letters from '**n**e**w l**ak**es**' and you get E, L, K and S – ELKS – the 'male creatures with bony appendages'.

If the wordplay indicates that you take the odd letters from part of the clue, then you take the first, third, fifth and seventh letters (and so on) from the appropriate words.

Regularly Placed Letters (other than odd or even)

The grid entry is produced from regularly placed letters in part of the clue, but not from every second letter as at the previous type.

 CLUE   *Winged creatures found regularly in kolas with locusts* (4)

SOLUTION   OWLS

Explanation: 'Found regularly' indicates that you have to take regularly placed letters from the clue to find the grid entry. If you take the second, sixth, tenth, and fourteenth letters of 'kolas with locusts', you get O, W, L and S. OWLS, which are 'winged creatures'.

Initials and Final Letters

The first or last letters of the indicated words are taken to produce the grid entry.

CLUE   *Vehicle can accelerate rapidly first of all* (3)

SOLUTION   CAR

Explanation: The definition is 'vehicle'. 'First of all' indicates that you have to take the first letters of each of the preceding words, which are 'can accelerate rapidly'. C, A and R gives CAR, which matches the definition 'vehicle'.

Specifically Placed Letters

Letters in certain positions in indicated words are taken to produce part of (or in a few cases) the whole of the grid entry.

CLUE *Dramas to perform on 5th of August* (5)

SOLUTION PLAYS

Explanation: Another word for 'perform' is 'play'. '5th of August' indicates that you have to take the fifth letter from the word 'August', which is S. When you add S to the end of 'play' you get PLAYS, which is another word for 'dramas', the definition.

Abbreviations, Numbers and Symbols

These are often used to indicate one or more letters in a solution.

CLUE *Hot, old, black surface beside fireplace* (3)

SOLUTION HOB

Explanation: H is a common abbreviation for 'hot', O is often used for 'old' and B is an abbreviation for 'black'. A HOB is a 'surface beside fireplace'.

CRYPTIC
INDICATORS

The more crosswords you do, the more chance you have of building up a memory bank of the various clue types and devices. It is rather like learning a foreign language – the more practice you have, the more proficient you become.

Given time and (prolonged) effort you will, we promise, turn from a Watson into a Holmes as you start solving puzzles before even having lit your morning pipe. A major step is to start seeing the clues within the clues. We call these 'cryptic indicators' and they are words or phrases that tell you what kind of puzzle you face.

Anagram Indicators

The words in this list tend to be concerned with movement and change, either directly, as in 'amended', 'different' and 'reordered', or indirectly, as in 'cuckoo', 'nervous' and 'off'. It is important to become familiar with the commonest anagram indicators because anagram clues can be some of the easiest to solve. If you search the web for 'cryptic crossword anagram indicators' you will find over 4000 sites, some of which list over 2000 words and phrases! Many of these lists are rather far-fetched and obscure, much like their compilers probably are, and editors and setters might not agree on which are acceptable and fair.

But in these recessionary days with cuts to the most fundamental public services looming, we do not want to be accused of excess and so have cut things down to a minimal 449 for you here.

abroad	all-round
acrobatically	altered
adapted	amended
adjusted	annoyed
affected	appalling
agitated	aroused
all at sea	arranged
all over the place	assorted

baffled	careless
bamboozled	carved (up)
bats	cavorting
battered	changed
becoming	chaotic
befuddled	chewed (up)
bemused	chopped (up)
bespoke	choppy
bewildered	churned
bizarre	circulating
blended	clobbered
blundering	clumsy
blurred	cock up (cock-up)
bogus	cocktail
boiling	collapsing
botched	collected
bothered	combustible
brewed	compiled
broadcast	complex
broken	complicated
buckled	components
bumbling	composed
bungled	compounded
bust	concocted
busy	confection
careering	confounded

confused
constituents
contrived
converted
convoluted
convulsed
corrected
corrupt
could be
cracked (up)
crackers
crackpot
crafted
cranky
crashed
crazy
crooked
crumbled
crushed
cuckoo
cultivated
damaged
dancing
dashed
dazed
dealt out

decomposed
demolished
destabilized
destroyed
deteriorating
devastated
developed
deviating
devious
diabolical
different
disarranged
disbanded
disconcerted
disguised
dishevelled
disintegrated
disjointed
dislocated
dismantled
disordered
disorganized
disorientated
dispersed
disrupted
dissolute

distorted
distraught
distressed
distributed
disturbed
diverted
dizzy
doctored
dodgy
dotty
doubtful
dreadful
drifting
drunk
dubious
duff
dynamic
eccentric
effervescent
elastic
emended
emerging from
engineered
entangled
entwined
erratic

erroneous
erupting
evolving
exchanged
excited
exploded
extraordinary
fabricated
fake
falsified
fashioned
fermented
feverish
fishy
flailing
flawed
flexible
flighty
flitting
floundering
flowing
fluctuating
fluid
fluttering
flying
forged

forming
frantic
free
frenetic
fresh
frisky
frolicsome
from
fudged
funny
gambolling
garbled
generated
giddy
groomed
ground
haphazard
hash
havoc
haywire
head over heels
hectic
helter skelter
higgledy-piggledy
hotchpotch
ill-assorted

impaired
imperfect
improvised
in a mess
in disarray
in discord
in error
in motion
incorrect
intoxicated
invalid
irregular
itinerant
jazzy
jittery
jockeying
jostled
juggled
jumbled
kind of
kneaded
lawless
lax
leaping
liberal
lively

loose
malleable
managed
mangled
manipulated
manoeuvred
marred
marshalled
mashed
masquerading
massaged
maybe
mayhem
meandering
medley
mélange
mêlée
melting
merry
messed
metamorphosed
minced
mingled
mischievous
misconstrued
misdirected

misguided
mishandled
misinterpreted
mismanaged
misplaced
misprinted
misrepresented
misshapen
misspelt
mistaken
mixed
mixture
mobile
modelled
modified
mongrel
moulded
moving
muddled
mussed
mutilated
mysterious
negotiated
nervous
new
novel

odd	random
off	realigned
ordered	rearranged
organized	reassembled
otherwise	rebuilt
out of order	recast
outrageous	recollected
pastiche	reconfigured
peculiar	reconstituted
perhaps	reconstructed
perturbed	recreated
phony	recycled
playing	redeployed
ploughed	redeveloped
possibly	rediscovered
potentially	redistributed
prancing	redrafted
preposterous	refashioned
processed	refined
producing	reformed
providing	regenerated
pummelled	rehashed
quaking	rejigged
quivering	remade
rambling	remedied
ramshackle	remodelled

renewed
renovated
reordered
reorganized
repackaged
replaced
repositioned
represented
reprocessed
resettled
reshaped
reshuffled
resolved
resorted
restless
restored
revamped
revised
reworked
rewritten
rocked
rollicking
rotten
rough
roving
ruffled

ruined
rum
sabotaged
salad
scattered
scrambled
scuffled
sculpted
seething
shaken
sham
shattered
shifted
shivering
shuffled
slapdash
smashed
somehow
sort of
sorted
spattered
spilt
spinning
spoilt
sporting
spread

sprinkled
squirming
staggering
stew
stirring
strange
straying
stumbling
suffering mishap
supple
suspect
swimming
swirling
tailored
terrible
thrown
tipsy
tottering
trained
tranfigured
transferred
transformed
translated
transposed
trembling
tumbledown

turbulent
turmoil
tweaked
twirling
twisted
unbalanced
uncommon
unexpected
unfamiliar
unhappy
unlikely
unnatural
unorthodox
unravelled
unrestrained
unrestricted
unruly
unscrambled
unsteady
untidy
unusual
unwound
upset
vacillating
vagrant
vague

varied
vibrating
vigorous
volatile
wandering
warped
wavering
waving
weird

whirling
wild
wobbling
worked
wrecked
writhing
wrong
zany

Reverse Direction Indicators

Some of these indicators should only appear in across clues, such as 'back', 'backing', 'going west' and 'turning'. Those found in down clues include 'rising', 'falling' and 'taken up'. Words such as 'reversed' and 'revolutionary' are widely used whether the entry is down or across.

about	going west
around	in recession
ascending	lifted
back(ing)	northern (erly)
backed up	over(turned)
(down clue)	reactionary
backward	rearing
capsized	returning
climbing	revolutionary
descending	rising
downwards	southern (erly)
dropping	taken up
elated	turning
elevated	upwards
falling	western
flipping	

Hidden Word Indicators

Clues in which the grid entry is concealed within the wordplay are usually easy to solve, so a working knowledge of these indicators can give you a good start in a crossword. Some more obvious examples of these are 'in', 'part of' and 'some', while others like 'boxing', 'bottles', 'parcels' and 'houses' are used with the intention of misleading you.

apparent in	in
bottles	includes
cans	involves
comes from	parcels
contributing to	part of
covers	partly
discovered in	resides in
emerges from	restrained by
encloses (ed by)	restricts
encompasses	shown in
found in	slice of
held by	some
houses	

Contracted Forms Indicators

When we call a word a contracted form, we mean
that it is a shortened version of a word or words, such
as 'promo' for 'promotion' and 'kinda' for 'kind of'.
Dictionaries sometimes call these short forms. They are
not used very often in cryptic crosswords but it is useful
to be able to recognize them when they occur. Then
you will know that 'in brief' may be an indicator of a
contracted form, and nothing to do with law or legal
matters.

contracted (to)	in short
contracting	reduced (to)
contracts (to)	shortened (to)
in brief	

Moving Letter Indicators

Wordplay sometimes indicates that a letter needs to be moved to provide the grid entry. 'Head dropping', for example, may suggest that the first letter of a word be moved to create the word to be written in the grid. As with the indicators for 'reverse direction', some indicators of moving letters apply only to down clues, for example 'rising', 'descending' and 'climbing'. This is also the case for 'boosted' which means 'raised'. Indicators like 'switching' and 'swapping' can be for across or down clues. 'Spooner's' indicates that the initial letters of two words should be swapped, as in 'sons of toil' for 'tons of soil'. The Reverend William Spooner, an English clergyman renowned for mistakenly swapping letters in this way, gave these verbal slips their name: spoonerisms.

boosted	rising
climbing	slipping
descending	Spooner's
dropping	swapping
exchanging	switching
falling	

Deletion Indicators

Deletion is the device that requires the solver to drop part of a word in order to create the grid entry. It is one of the easier devices to use and so it has many indicators. Some are easy to understand, for example 'scrapped', 'omitted' and 'taken away'. Others are more obscure, such as 'Manx', which means that the last letter of a word is to be removed, because Manx cats have no tail! Strictly speaking 'Manx' should start with a capital letter, which is not a problem when it is the first word in the clue. However, a little bit of 'setter's licence' would allow it to appear elsewhere in a clue without the initial capital letter.

abandoned	cockney (missing h)
abridged	curtailed
absconding	deadheaded
absent	decaudated
away	defaced
banned	departs (ed)(ing)
barred	discarded
binned	discounted
blotted out	dismissed
cast	dropped
chucked	East End (no h)
clipped	eclipsed

41

ejected	obliterated
endless(ly)	obscured
eschewed	off
evicted	omitted
excised	out
excluded (ing)	peeled
flees (ing)	polled
guillotined	reduced
gutted	scrapped
headless	scratched
heaved (ing)	scrubbed
ignored	shelled
in Spitalfields (no h)	shorn
in Whitechapel (no h)	short (ened)
incomplete	splits
left	stripped
lopped	subtracted (ing)
lost	taken away
Manx	topless
masked	trashed
mislaid	unfinished
missing	veiled
not allowed	without
obfuscated	

Substituted Letter Indicators

Sometimes a letter suggested by the wordplay must be changed to form the grid entry An example of this is 'Scour new opening for tomb', where changing the first letter of 'tomb' provides the answer 'comb'. Most of these indicators are self-explanatory, but it is worth mentioning 'afore' and 'inform'. These words can be broken up into pieces: 'afore' becomes 'a for e' and 'inform' becomes 'in for m'. These can be used as indicators of substituted letters in a clue: 'substitute the letter a for the letter e' (afore) and 'substitute the letters in for m' (inform). However, some setters and editors would consider these unfair, and would not accept any word that contains 'for' within it as an indicator of a substituted letter.

afore (a for e)	in lieu of
becomes	in place of
change of	instead of
changed to	replaces
exchanged for	swapped for
for	switched for
inform (in for m)	

Archaic Indicators

Most of the indicators in this list are easy to understand, but there are one or two surprises. The best-known meaning of 'pristine', for example, is 'pure and unspoilt', but it can also mean 'original', 'former' and 'belonging to the earliest time'. 'Hoary', as in 'a hoary old chestnut' (meaning a joke that everyone has heard), also means 'ancient'. The French word 'passé', meaning 'out of date', has been imported into English. Accents are generally included in clues but ignored in grid entries.

ancient	of yore
archaic	old
bygone	old world
defunct	once
disused	outdated
Edmund's	passé
Ed's (Spenser)	(in the) past
ere-now	previously
extinct	pristine
(in) former (times)	Shakespeare's
historic	Shakespearean
hoary	Spenser's
in olden times	the Bard's
long gone	(Shakespeare's)
lost	veteran
no longer	was
obsolete	Will's (Shakespeare's)

Container and Contents Indicators

Some words may not mean what they appear to mean. A good example of this is 'without', which can mean 'deprived of' but can also mean 'outside'. 'Bottles' is a very devious and misleading indicator, as on first reading it seems to indicate a plural noun. But 'bottle' can also be a verb meaning 'to enclose in a bottle', so 'bottles' can actually mean 'encloses'. Another indicator of a container and contents device is 'bandage', which indicates wrapping one object round another.

about
absorbing
accommodating
adopting
around
bandages
bearing
besetting
besieging
blocks
boarding
bottles
boxing
cans
captivating

carrying
carts
cases
catching
caught by
clipping
consuming
containing
contains
conveying
covering
digesting
dividing
dressing
drinking

eating
embracing
encasing
enfolds
engaging
ensnaring
entertaining
enthralling
espousing
filling
frames
harnesses
held by
holds
houses
hugging
humping
imbibes
including
inflated
  (containing air)
ingesting
investing
keeping
limits
lining
necking

netting
obstructs
occupying
overdrawn (in red)
packing
parcelling
ports
restrains
restricts
retired (in bed)
sandwiches
separating
splits
splitting
sporting
stops
straddling
surrounded by
surrounding
swallowing
takes in
toting
trapping
wearing
without
wrapping

Homophone (sound device) Indicators

A homophone is a word that sounds like another word, even though they are spelt differently, for example 'rein', 'rain' and 'reign'. There are many groups of two or three or even more homophones in English and crossword setters love them! Homophone indicators can include any term that indicates the sound of a word, including potentially misleading ones such as 'pipe' and 'spout'. Both of these verbs can mean 'to speak' but that meaning is not the first one you would think of for either of them, so beware of 'piped' and 'spouted'.

articulated	phonetically
breathed	piped
broadcast	reported
called	said
hear (d) (ing)	so to speak
in conversation	sound
intoned	spoken
listened to	spouted
mouthed	stated
noised	sung
on the blower	voiced
on the phone	whispered
on the radio	

Initial and Final Letters Indicators

Setters often have to indicate one or more individual letters in wordplay. When just one letter is required, something like 'initially' or 'finally' can be used for the first or last letter. Any kind of opening or ending could be used, which is why 'overture' and 'bottom' are included. 'Overture' is the piece played at the beginning of an opera and 'bottom' can indicate the last letter in a down entry.

at last	first of all
beginning of	foremost
borders	foundation
bottom	front of
bounds	Gateshead
cap (s)	head of
crown (s)	initially
debut	intro
determination of	introduction
edges	introductory
end of	last of
endings	last of all
eventually	leader of
extremes	limits
finally	margins
finishes	onset of

openings   primes
origin (s)   rims
overture (s)   start (s) of
peripherally   top of
preliminaries   ultimately
primary

Regularly Placed Letters
(other than odd or even)

Although straightforward alternate letters are those most likely to be indicated in standard cryptic crosswords of average difficulty, setters may often select every third or fourth letter, in which case 'intermittently' won't necessarily mean every odd or even letter.

found at intervals in
found regularly in
intermittently

taken at intervals from
taken regularly from

Odd or Even Letters

'Odds' or 'evens' must mean every other letter.
Watch out for 'odds' though, for it could relate to
betting odds and actually be referring to 'SP' (which is
an abbreviation for 'starting price'). Some indicators
such as 'intermittently' may be used either for alternate
letters or for other intervals between letters. It is for the
solver to determine which is intended, by noting how
many letters are needed for the grid entry.

alternately
at intervals
even ones from/in
evenly (discarded)
every other from/in
intermittently

odd ones from/in
oddly (discarded)
odds
regularly (discarded)
unevenly

Dialect and Foreign Words Indicators

Cockney pronunciation is often used in crosswords to indicate a dropped H at the start of a word and, less often, a missing G from the end of a word. Scots or Yorkshire terms both qualify as 'northern'. Simple words from other languages are often included, the most common being 'the French' which can represent LE, LA, or LES (which are all ways of writing 'the' in French). Less common are 'a German' (EIN or EINE, which are German for 'a') 'the Italian' (IL, LO, LA, I, GLI or LE which are Italian words meaning 'the') and 'the Spanish' (EL, LA, LOS or LAS, all of which mean 'the').

cockney (missing h)	in Whitechapel (no h)
East End (missing h)	Italian
French	locally
German	northern
in places	Senor (man's name)
in Spitalfields (no h)	Senorita (girl's name)
in the country	Spanish

Specifically Placed Letters

'Colin essentially' could indicate L or OLI. The essence
of this is that you need to use the central letter or letters
of the word, and you have to work out how many you
need from the rest of the wordplay in the clue.

'Beethoven's ninth' refers to the letter N, the ninth letter
in his name.

Beethoven's ninth (n)   middle of
centre of   nucleus of
core of   second, third, fourth
essentially   (and so on)
heart of

Shortened Forms Indicators

Setters may sometimes indicate that a shortened form of a word is needed, such as 'lab' for 'laboratory' or 'labrador' (the dog). A devious setter may reverse this idea by using something like 'I expanded' where the entry required is 'independent'. 'I' is a common abbreviation for 'independent' and the setter is asking the solver to expand the abbreviation 'I' to its full form.

briefly	little
in brief	short (ened)

Misleading Single Word Definitions

Crossword setters love to use tricky definitions within
wordplay, and sometimes even like to include themselves
in the clue. So a 'setter' appearing within a clue is not
necessarily a dog. When indicating the creator of the
puzzle, 'setter' may mean 'me' or 'I', or even the setter's
name.

Another common device is the one-word definition of
the answer. A 'swimmer' is almost always a fish and a
'banker', rather than someone who works for Barclays,
is sometimes a river. A river, however, is more often a
'flower' (something that 'flows', not the thing you buy
in bunches).

Watch out for 'specs', which can indicate 'oo'
(supposedly resembling the frames of a pair of glasses),
and other indicators that depend on what the letters
look like.

admission of (I'm)	engagement (battle)
banker (river)	flier (bird)
bread (money)	flower (river)
butter (ram, goat)	his (greetings)
claim by or of (I'm)	lower (cattle)
declaration of (I'm)	my (setter of puzzle)
empty (containing o)	number (drug)

pen (writer)
potter (snooker
  player)
ready (money)
retired (in bed)
rhino (money)
scorer (composer)

setter (of puzzle –
  not a dog!)
spec(tacle)s (oo)
swimmer (fish)
tin (money)
winger (bird)
writer (setter of puzzle)

Entry Direction in Across Clues

If the setter indicates that an across clue is 'going west', this could be a way of saying that there is a reversal involved. We write from left to right or, in terms of direction, from west to east. Therefore 'going west' can be a hint about reversing the order of something in the clue to find the grid entry.

about	going west
around	reverse
backward	western (ly)
forward	

Entry Direction in Down Clues

'West' and 'western' won't work for a down clue because down answers are written from top to bottom. In down clues you are likely to find references to 'rising' and 'falling'.

ascending	going down
climbing	going up
descending	northerly
dropping	southerly
falling	

Position of Parts

Those letters or words that make up the required solution may be placed alongside each other, as in 'One playing recordings of a bird by a river' for DEEJAY ('Dee' is a river and 'jay' is a bird). In this clue 'by' is a linking word meaning 'at the side of'. The words in the following list are generally links like this, although they may be less obvious than 'by', 'on' or 'over'. In down clues, words indicating 'support' may be used when one part is to be placed on top of another. But be careful. 'River supports' could be a clue for TEES ('Tees' is a river and 'tees' are the pegs used to support golf balls). The word 'by' may indicate the letter X (as used in measurements, for example 6m x 10m). In a down clue, a word may be described as 'supporting' if it appears under another word. However, a word that is on top of another word may be considered to be an 'oppressor'.

above	in support of
alongside	on
bearing	oppressing
below	over
beneath	supporting
by	

Abbreviations

Words which have abbreviated forms abound in the wordplay of cryptic clues. It pays to become familiar with as many of these as possible. Here are some examples, most of which are in common use, but we have included a few to show how devious setters of cryptic crosswords can be!

across = AC

born = B

caught = C, CT

degree = BA, MA

doctor = DR, MD

English = E

fifty = L (*Roman numeral*)

good = G

hospital = H

I have = IVE

knight = K

last letter = Z

many = C, D, L, M (*Roman numerals*)

new = N;

opponent = E, N, S, W (*in card games such as whist*)

parking = P
queen = ER, Q
run out = RO
special = S, SP
time = HR, MIN, T
used = SH (*second-hand*)
victory = V
with = W
yard = Y, YD
zero = O

USEFUL

LISTS

Regardless of how many tips and tricks you master, you will still come unstuck if you simply don't know the answer word. Crossword answers (particular those of certain setters) have a tendency to every so often flee into obscure corners of the lexicon. In these instances, books like ***Bradford's Crossword Solver's Dictionary*** can be an invaluable source of unfamiliar words.

What follows are some lists of the groups of words that crop up most often in answers. We've omitted a few of the most popular lists (like cities, mountains and currencies) because they are readily available elsewhere. What we've included is a pageant of the usual unusual suspects.

Enjoy; you need never feel listless again.

Alcoholic Drink

4 LETTERS
dram
grog
kvas
mead
saké
soma

5 LETTERS
cider
glogg
kvass
negus
quass
toddy

6 LETTERS
busera
caudle
chaser

frappé
posset
pulque
samshu
waragi

7 LETTERS
Campari
Cinzano
liqueur
Martini
shooter
slammer
apéritif
cocktail

8 LETTERS
Dubonnet
gluhwein
palm wine

rice wine
skokiaan
vermouth

9 LETTERS
hard cider
hippocras
snakebite

10 LETTERS
ginger wine
malt liquor
mulled wine
spruce beer

11 LETTERS
Irish coffee

12 LETTERS
Gaelic coffee

Arable Crops

To help you cotton on.

3 LETTERS
pea
rye
yam

4 LETTERS
bean
beet
corn
flax
hemp
jute
kail
kale
leek
milo
oats
okra
rape
rice
taro

5 LETTERS
colza
fonio
maize
olive
onion
spelt
swede
wheat

6 LETTERS
adzuki
barley
carrot
celery
cotton
endive
lentil
manioc
millet
peanut
pepper
potato

quinoa
radish
squash
tomato
turnip

7 LETTERS
alfalfa
cabbage
cassava
chicory
lettuce
linseed
lucerne
oilseed
parsnip
pumpkin
shallot
sorghum
soy bean
spinach
tobacco

8 LETTERS
broccoli
chickpea
cucumber
fava bean
lima bean
mung bean
rutabaga
rye-grass
soya bean
sweet pea

9 LETTERS
artichoke
asparagus
aubergine
broad bean

buckwheat
courgette
kafir corn
milo maize
pinto bean
sugar beet
sugar cane
sunflower
sweetcorn
triticale

10 LETTERS
butter bean
durum wheat
kaffir corn
kidney bean

opium poppy
runner bean

11 LETTERS
cauliflower
haricot bean
horseradish
oilseed rape
sweet potato

12 LETTERS
black-eyed pea
mangelwurzel
oil palm fruit

14 LETTERS
Brussels sprout
castor-oil plant

Ball Games

Making crosswords a mere bagatelle.

4 LETTERS
golf
pool

5 LETTERS
fives

6 LETTERS
boules
hockey
soccer
squash
tennis

7 LETTERS
bowling
croquet
hurling
netball

pinball
pyramid
snooker

8 LETTERS
baseball
football
goalball
handball
korfball
lacrosse
pushball
rounders
Subbuteo

9 LETTERS
badminton
bagatelle

billiards
crazy golf
paintball
punchball

10 LETTERS
volleyball

15 LETTERS
Australian Rules

16 LETTERS
American
    football
Canadian
    football
piggy in the
    middle

Ballet Steps and Terms

To help you answer with aplomb.

3 LETTERS
pas

4 LETTERS
jeté
plié

5 LETTERS
adage
battu
brisé
coupé
decor
passé
tombé

6 LETTERS
adagio
aplomb
ballon
chassé
croisé
dégagé
ecarté
en l'air

failli
ouvert
pointe
relevé

7 LETTERS
allegro
allongé
balancé
ciseaux
déboulé
échappé
emboîté
soutenu
turn-out

8 LETTERS
abstract
assemblé
attitude
ballonné
ballotté
batterie
cabriole

demi-plié
en dedans
en dehors
en pointe
figurant
glissade
pas coupé
sickling
sur place
temps lié
toe-dance

9 LETTERS
arabesque
ballerina
battement
cou-de-pied
détournée
développée
elevation
entrechat
pas de chat
pas de deux
pirouette

raccourci
temps levé
variation

10 LETTERS
changement
demi-pointe
en couronne
foudroyant
grand écart
grande plié

pas échappé
pas ciseaux
pas de brisé
soubresaut
tour en l'air

11 LETTERS
ballet blanc
contretemps
pas ballotté
pas de bourée

pas de chassé
ports de bras
rond de jambe
terre à terre

12 LETTERS
ballet de cour
croisé devant
enchaînement
gargouillade

Beans and other Pulses

Bobby's a dhal old bean.

3 LETTERS
red

4 LETTERS
dhal
gram
lima
mung
navy
soya

5 LETTERS
black
bobby
broad
field
green
pinto

6 LETTERS
adzuki
butter
French
kidney
lentil
runner
string

7 LETTERS
haricot
snow pea

8 LETTERS
borlotti
chick pea
garbanzo
split pea

9 LETTERS
black-eyed
cannelini
flageolet
mangetout
petit pois
pigeon pea
puy lentil
red kidney
red lentil

11 LETTERS
green lentil

12 LETTERS
black-eyed pea
marrowfat pea
sugar snap pea

Beetles

What shall it bee: dung or furniture?

3 LETTERS
bee
dor
May
oil

4 LETTERS
bark
dung
flea
gold
huhu
June
king
leaf
pill
rose
rove
stag

5 LETTERS
bacon
black
click

snout
tiger
water

6 LETTERS
carpet
chafer
diving
elater
ground
larder
May bug
museum
potato
scarab
sexton
weevil

7 LETTERS
Asiatic
blister
burying
cabinet
carrion

firefly
goldbug
goliath
June bug
ladybug
leather
soldier
vedalia

8 LETTERS
ambrosia
cardinal
Colorado
curculio
glow-worm
Hercules
Japanese
ladybird
Māori bug
skipjack
snapping
tortoise

9 LETTERS
carpet bug
Christmas
furniture
goldsmith
kekerengu
longicorn
pea weevil
scavenger

timberman
whirligig

10 LETTERS
bean weevil
boll weevil
bombardier
churchyard
cockchafer
deathwatch

long-horned
rhinoceros
rose chafer
Spanish fly

11 LETTERS
bloody-nosed

16 LETTERS
devil's coach-
horse

Biscuits

Don't let it drive you crackers.

4 LETTERS
farl
rusk

5 LETTERS
matzo
wafer

6 LETTERS
cookie

7 LETTERS
bannock
bourbon
cracker
fairing
oatcake
pretzel
ratafia
rich tea

8 LETTERS
amaretti
cracknel
flapjack
hardtack
macaroon

9 LETTERS
abernethy
digestive
garibaldi
ginger nut
Jaffa cake
lebkuchen
petit four
shortcake

10 LETTERS
Bath Oliver
brandy snap
crispbread
Florentine
ginger snap
love letter
sea biscuit
shortbread
tea biscuit

11 LETTERS
soda biscuit

12 LETTERS
caramel wafer
cream cracker
langue de chat
pilot biscuit
ship's biscuit
water biscuit

13 LETTERS
Empire biscuit
graham cracker

14 LETTERS
gingerbread man
Tararua biscuit

15 LETTERS
captain's biscuit

16 LETTERS
sweetmeal biscuit

18 LETTERS
chocolate
  digestive

Bones

Are you using your cranium?

3 LETTERS
rib

4 LETTERS
ulna

5 LETTERS
anvil
costa
femur
hyoid
ilium
incus
pubis
skull
spine
talus
tibia
wrist

6 LETTERS
carpal
carpus
coccyx
cuboid

fibula
hallux
hammer
pelvis
radius
sacrum
stapes
tarsal
tarsus

7 LETTERS
cranium
ethmoid
hipbone
humerus
ischium
kneecap
malleus
maxilla
patella
phalanx
scapula
sternum
stirrup

8 LETTERS
backbone
brainpan
clavicle
heel bone
mandible
shinbone
sphenoid
vertebra

9 LETTERS
anklebone
calcaneus
cheekbone
thighbone

10 LETTERS
astragalus
breastbone
collarbone
metacarpal
metatarsal
metatarsus

11 LETTERS
frontal bone
lower jawbone
parietal bone
spinal column
temporal bone
upper jawbone

13 LETTERS
occipital bone
shoulder blade
zygomatic bone

14 LETTERS
innominate bone

15 LETTERS
vertebral
  column

Bottles

A list for when your mind is flagon.

5 LETTERS
flask
gourd
phial

6 LETTERS
carboy
caster
flacon
flagon
lagena
stubby

7 LETTERS
ampulla

8 LETTERS
decanter
demijohn
half-jack
screw top

9 LETTERS
miniature

10 LETTERS
pycnometer
soda siphon

11 LETTERS
vinaigrette
water bottle

12 LETTERS
Nansen bottle
Woulfe bottle

13 LETTERS
feeding bottle

14 LETTERS
hot-water bottle

Breeds of Cat

Is there room in the grid for a Bengal leopard?

3 LETTERS
Rex

4 LETTERS
Manx

5 LETTERS
tabby

6 LETTERS
Angora
Havana

7 LETTERS
Burmese
Persian
ragdoll
Siamese
Turkish

9 LETTERS
Himalayan
Maine coon

10 LETTERS
Abyssinian

11 LETTERS
colourpoint
Russian blue

13 LETTERS
Bengal leopard
tortoiseshell

Breeds of Dog

It Saluki we gave you these pointers to answer the setter.

3 LETTERS
lab
pug

4 LETTERS
barb
chow
puli

5 LETTERS
Akita
boxer
cairn
corgi
husky
spitz

6 LETTERS
beagle
borzoi
briard
collie
kelpie
poodle
Saluki

setter
sleuth
talbot
vizsla

7 LETTERS
basenji
bouvier
bulldog
griffon
harrier
Maltese
mastiff
pointer
Samoyed
Scottie
sheltie
shih-tzu
spaniel
terrier
whippet

8 LETTERS
Alsatian
chow-chow
coach dog
Doberman
elkhound
foxhound
keeshond
komondor
Labrador
malamute
malemute
papillon

9 LETTERS
chihuahua
coonhound
dachshund
Dalmatian
deerhound
Eskimo dog
Great Dane
greyhound
Lhasa apso

Pekingese
red setter
retriever
schnauzer
staghound
St Bernard
wolfhound

10 LETTERS
bloodhound
Bruxellois
fox terrier
Pomeranian
Rottweiler
schipperke
Weimaraner
Welsh corgi

11 LETTERS
Afghan hound
basset hound
bull mastiff
bull terrier
carriage dog
Irish setter
rough collie
sleuthhound

12 LETTERS
Border collie
Newfoundland
Saint Bernard

13 LETTERS
cocker spaniel
English setter
Scotch terrier

14 LETTERS
German
  shepherd
Irish
  wolfhound
pit bull terrier

15 LETTERS
Airedale terrier
golden retriever
Highland terrier

16 LETTERS
Doberman
  pinscher
Yorkshire terrier

17 LETTERS
Jack Russell
  terrier

18 LETTERS
Rhodesian
  ridgeback

Cakes and Pastries

A tart re-torte delivered with éclair is often the best answer.

4 LETTERS
tart

5 LETTERS
donut
scone
torte

6 LETTERS
eclair
gateau
jumbal
jumble
kuchen
muffin
parkin
yumyum

7 LETTERS
baklava
brownie
cruller
crumpet
cupcake
kruller

pancake
rum baba
stollen
teacake

8 LETTERS
black bun
doughnut
dumpling
flapjack
meringue
mince pie
pandowdy
rock cake
seedcake
teabread
turnover

9 LETTERS
angel cake
cream cake
cream puff
drop scone
fairy cake
fruitcake
fudge cake

Genoa cake
kugelhopf
lamington
lardy cake
layer cake
madeleine
panettone
petit four
pound cake
queencake
Sally Lunn
swiss roll
tipsy cake

10 LETTERS
almond cake
carrot cake
cherry cake
coffee kiss
Dundee cake
Eccles cake
frangipane
johnny cake
koeksister
ladyfinger

79

marble cake
simnel cake
sponge cake

11 LETTERS
Banbury cake
coconut cake
gingerbread
hot cross bun
Linzer torte
Madeira cake
profiterole
wedding cake

12 LETTERS
Bakewell tart
Danish pastry
French pastry
millefeuille
sandwich cake
singing hinny
sponge finger

13 LETTERS
angel food cake
chocolate cake
Christmas cake
Genoese sponge

14 LETTERS
Battenburg cake
devil's food cake
Selkirk bannock
upside-down
  cake
Victoria sponge

17 LETTERS
Black forest
  gateau

Car Parts

No need to stay an ammeter solver.

3 LETTERS
fan
top

4 LETTERS
axle
body
boot
bulb
coil
cowl
door
fuse
gear
hood
horn
jack
lock
plug
roof
seat
sump
tank
trim

tyre
wing

5 LETTERS
brake
choke
crank
light
pedal
valve
wheel

6 LETTERS
air bag
big end
bonnet
bumper
clutch
engine
fascia
fender
gasket
grille
heater

hubcap
piston
points
towbar
window

7 LETTERS
ammeter
ashtray
battery
bearing
chassis
exhaust
fan belt
fog lamp
fuse box
gearbox
hard top
mud flap
oil pump
springs
starter
sunroof
wing nut

8 LETTERS
brake pad
camshaft
cylinder
demister
dipstick
flywheel
ignition
manifold
odometer
radiator
seat belt
silencer
tailgate
tailpipe

9 LETTERS
crankcase
dashboard
fuel gauge
gear lever
gearshift
generator
handbrake
indicator

little end
milometer
oil filter
petrol cap
rear light
taillight
wheel trim
alternator

10 LETTERS
brake light
crankshaft
disc brakes
door handle
driveshaft
mileometer
petrol tank
safety belt
spare wheel
suspension
torsion bar
wing mirror

11 LETTERS
accelerator

anti-roll bar
carburettor
distributor
hazard light
luggage rack
numberplate
parcel shelf
petrol gauge
speedometer
transmission

13 LETTERS
connecting rod
steering wheel

14 LETTERS
automatic
  choke

15 LETTERS
windscreen
  wiper

16 LETTERS
glove
  compartment

Cheeses

For when the setter drives you emmental.

3 LETTERS
Oka

4 LETTERS
Brie
Edam
feta
yarg

5 LETTERS
Caboc
Derby
Esrom
Gouda
quark
Samsø

6 LETTERS
Cantal
chèvre
Dunlop
Ermite
Romano

7 LETTERS
Chaumes
Cheddar
crowdie
fontina
Gjetost
Gruyère
Havarti
mycella
ricotta
sapsago
Stilton

8 LETTERS
Bel Paese
blue vein
Cheshire
Emmental
muenster
Parmesan
pecorino
Taleggio
Tornegus
Vacherin
vignotte
83

9 LETTERS
Blue Vinny
Camembert
Emmenthal
Jarlsberg
Leicester
Limburger
mousetrap
Port-Salut
pot cheese
provolone
Reblochon
Roquefort
Sage Derby
Saint Agur

10 LETTERS
blue cheese
Blue Vinney
Bonchester
Caerphilly
Cambazolla
canestrato
curd cheese

Danish blue
Dolcelatte
Gorgonzola
Lanark Blue
Lancashire
mascarpone
mozzarella
Neufchâtel
Red Windsor

11 LETTERS
Blue Stilton
cream cheese

Dunsyre Blue
goats' cheese
Ribblesdale
wensleydale

12 LETTERS
Bavarian blue
Bleu de Bresse
caciocavallo
fromage frais
Monterey jack
Red Leicester

13 LETTERS
Bleu d'Auvergne
cottage cheese

14 LETTERS
Blue
  Shropshire
Stinking Bishop

16 LETTERS
Double
  Gloucester

Cosmetics

Look beneath the concealer.

4 LETTERS
kohl

5 LETTERS
henna
rouge
toner

6 LETTERS
eye gel

7 LETTERS
blusher
bronzer
cologne
fake tan
hair gel
lip balm
mascara
perfume

8 LETTERS
cleanser
eye cream
eyeliner
face mask
face pack
lip gloss
lip liner
lipstick
panstick
spray tan

9 LETTERS
body spray
cold cream
concealer
deodorant
exfoliant
eye shadow
face cream
hair serum
hair spray
hand cream

10 LETTERS
aftershave
body butter
face powder
foundation
hair colour
nail polish
night cream

11 LETTERS
greasepaint
hair lacquer
highlighter
moisturizer
nail varnish

12 LETTERS
body spritzer

13 LETTERS
eyebrow pencil

14 LETTERS
antiperspirant

Cricket Terms

Stumped?

2 LETTERS
in

3 LETTERS
bat
bye
cut
out
pad
run
six

4 LETTERS
bail
ball
bowl
duck
edge
four
hook
over
pull
seam
slip

spin
wide

5 LETTERS
Ashes
catch
drive
extra
glide
gully
mid on
pitch
stump
sweep
swing

6 LETTERS
appeal
bowled
bowler
bumper
caught
covers
crease

doosra
glance
googly
leg bye
long on
mid off
no ball
on side
opener
run out
single
umpire
wicket
yorker

7 LETTERS
batsman
bouncer
century
declare
fielder
fine leg
innings
leg side

leg slip
long leg
long off
off side
off spin
stumped

8 LETTERS
boundary
chinaman
follow on
full toss
leg break
off break
short leg
third man
Twenty20

9 LETTERS
fieldsman
hit wicket
mid wicket
square leg
test match

10 LETTERS
cover point
extra cover
fast bowler
maiden over
off-spinner
silly mid on
twelfth man

11 LETTERS
silly mid off

12 LETTERS
wicketkeeper

13 LETTERS
nightwatchman

14 LETTERS
opening
 batsman

15 LETTERS
leg before
 wicket

Dances

A list for when you're stuck in limbo.

3 LETTERS
hay
hey
jig

4 LETTERS
bump
haka
hora
hula
jive
jota
juba
kolo
mosh
pogo
reel

5 LETTERS
bogle
brawl
carol
conga
galop

gigue
limbo
mambo
polka
round
rumba
salsa
samba
shake
skank
stomp
tango
twist
volta
waltz

6 LETTERS
bolero
boogie
boston
branle
cancan
cha-cha
german

hustle
maxixe
minuet
nautch
pavane
redowa
shimmy
Zapata

7 LETTERS
beguine
bourrée
calypso
carioca
czardas
foxtrot
gavotte
hoedown
lambada
lancers
ländler
mazurka
Moresco
Morisco

musette
one-step
roundel
saunter
shuffle
two-step

8 LETTERS
boogaloo
bunny hug
cachucha
cakewalk
chaconne
courante
fan dance
fandango
flamenco
galliard
hornpipe
hula-hula
macarena
poi dance
tap dance
war dance

9 LETTERS
allemande
barn dance
bossa nova
breakdown
butterfly
cha-cha-cha
clog dance
cotillion
ecossaise
folk dance
jitterbug
line dance
paso doble
pole dance
polonaise
quadrille
quickstep
ring-shout
roundelay

10 LETTERS
charleston
snake dance
strathspey
sword dance

11 LETTERS
morris dance

13 LETTERS
Highland fling

14 LETTERS
formation dance
strip the willow
Sir Roger de
  Coverley

21 LETTERS
Dashing White
  Sergeant

Deserts

For when your mind's a deserted blank.

4 LETTERS
Gobi
Thar

6 LETTERS
Gibson
Libyan
Mohave
Mojave
Nubian
Sahara

7 LETTERS
Arabian
Atacama
Kara Kum

8 LETTERS
Kalahari
Kyzyl Kum

9 LETTERS
Dasht-e-Lut

10 LETTERS
Great Sandy
Rub'al Khali

11 LETTERS
Death Valley

13 LETTERS
Great Victoria

15 LETTERS
Taklimakan
 Shama

Fabrics

Don't knit your brows.

3 LETTERS
fur
net
say

4 LETTERS
ciré
cord
drab
duck
felt
huck
jean
knit
lace
lamé
lawn
mull
shag
silk
tick
wool

5 LETTERS
baize
batik
beige

crape
crepe
denim
frisé
gunny
honan
khaki
linen
lisle
Lurex™
Lycra™
moiré
ninon
Orlon™
panne
piqué
plush
poult
rayon
satin
scrim
serge
stuff

surah
surat
tabby
tammy
terry
toile
tulle
tweed
twill
voile
alpaca

6 LETTERS
armure
barège
battik
bouclé
burlap
calico
camlet
chintz
cilice
cloqué
cotton

cyprus
Dacron
damask
dimity
Dralon
etamin
faille
fleece
frieze
gloria
jersey
kincob
madras
melton
mohair
moreen
muslin
nankin
Oxford

pongee
poplin
russet
tartan
velure
velvet

7 LETTERS
brocade
cambric
fishnet
flannel
fustian
galatea
gingham
Gore-Tex™
hessian
oilskin
worsted

8 LETTERS
buckskin
corduroy
cretonne
gossamer
lambskin
marocain
moleskin

9 LETTERS
crinoline
tarpaulin

10 LETTERS
broadcloth
India print

11 LETTERS
cheesecloth
Harris Tweed

Famous Battles

Watch the answers come Flodden in.

4 LETTERS
Jena
Zama
Alamo

5 LETTERS
Boyne
Bulge
Crécy
Issus
Kursk
Pydna
Somme
Ypres

6 LETTERS
Actium
Arnhem
Barnet
Cannae
Imphal
Lützen
Naseby
Sadová

Sadowa
Shiloh
Tobruk
Verdun
Wagram

7 LETTERS
Bautzen
Britain
Bull Run
Falkirk
Flodden
Leipzig
Lepanto
Marengo
Plassey
Plataea
Poltava
Salamis
Sempach
Trenton
Vitoria

8 LETTERS
Atlantic
Blenheim
Borodino
Culloden
Edgehill
Hastings
Inkerman
Jemappes
Le Cateau
Manassas
Mantinea
Marathon
Navarino
Omdurman
Philippi
Waterloo

9 LETTERS
Abukir Bay
Agincourt
Balaclava
Balaklava
El Alamein

Ladysmith
Leyte Gulf
Mantineia
Ramillies
Sedgemoor
Trafalgar

10 LETTERS
Aboukir Bay
Austerlitz
Bunker Hill
Gettysburg
Quatre Bras
Shipka Pass
Stalingrad
Tannenberg
Tewkesbury

11 LETTERS
Bannockburn
Belleau Wood
Dien Bien Phu
Guadalcanal
Hohenlinden
Marston Moor
Prestonpans
Saint-Mihiel
Thermopylae

12 LETTERS
Roncesvalles

13 LETTERS
Bosworth Field
Killiecrankie
Little Bighorn
Passchendaele
Stamford
   Bridge
Stirling Bridge

15 LETTERS
Missionary
   Ridge
Plains of
   Abraham

Flower Parts

To help your solving flourish.

5 LETTERS
calyx
ovary
ovule
petal
sepal
spike
stalk
style
torus
umbel

6 LETTERS
anther
carpel
corymb
pistil

raceme
spadix
stamen
stigma

7 LETTERS
corolla
nectary
panicle
pedicel

8 LETTERS
filament
perianth
thalamus

9 LETTERS
capitulum

dichasium
gynoecium

10 LETTERS
androecium
connective
floral axis
pollen tube
receptacle

11 LETTERS
monochasium

12 LETTERS
articulation

15 LETTERS
microsporangium

Gemstones

A hiddenite answer?

3 LETTERS
jet

4 LETTERS
jade
onyx
opal
ruby
sard

5 LETTERS
agate
balas
beryl
topaz

6 LETTERS
garnet
jasper
morion
plasma
pyrope
quartz
sphene
spinel

zircon

7 LETTERS
cat's-eye
citrine
diamond
emerald
girasol
girosol
helidor
jacinth
jadeite
kunzite
peridot
sardine

8 LETTERS
adularia
amethyst
corundum
diopside
fire opal
girasole
hawk's-eye

hyacinth
melanite
sapphire
sardonyx
sunstone
titanite

9 LETTERS
almandine
amazonite
andradite
aventurin
black opal
cairngorm
carnelian
cymophane
demantoid
hessonite
hiddenite
liver opal
moonstone
morganite
moss agate
rhodolite

rubellite
spodumene
turquoise
uvarovite

10 LETTERS
andalusite
aquamarine
avanturine
aventurine
bloodstone
chalcedony
chrysolite
heliotrope
indicolite
indigolite
odontolite

rose quartz
staurolite
topazolite
tourmaline

11 LETTERS
alexandrite
chrysoberyl
chrysoprase
lapis lazuli
smoky quartz
spessartite
vesuvianite

12 LETTERS
Colorado ruby
grossularite
Spanish topaz

13 LETTERS
bone turquoise
Colorado topaz
water sapphire
white sapphire

15 LETTERS
Oriental
  emerald

17 LETTERS
Oriental
  almandine

20 LETTERS
Madagascar
  aquamarine
New Zealand
  greenstone

Gods

One of them's got to be right.

2 LETTERS
Ra
Re

3 LETTERS
Eos
Hel
Pan
Set
Sol
Tyr

4 LETTERS
Agni
Ares
Devi
Eris
Eros
Frey
Gaea
Gaia
Hebe
Hela
Hera
Idun

Iris
Isis
Jove
Juno
Kali
Kama
Loki
Luna
Maat
Mars
Maya
Nike
Odin
Ptah
Rama
Rhea
Siva
Thor
Tyrr
Zeus

5 LETTERS
Aegir
Aesir

Bragi
Ceres
Cupid
Diana
Durga
Fates
Flora
Freya
Freyr
Frigg
Hades
Horae
Horus
Hymen
Indra
Janus
Lares
Momus
Njord
Norns
Othin
Pluto
Shiva
Thoth

Ushas
Vanir
Venus

6 LETTERS
Aeolus
Amen-Ra
Anubis
Apollo
Athene
Aurora
Balder
Boreas
Brahma
Cronos
Cybele
Faunus
Freyja
Frigga
Ganesa
Graces
Hathor
Hecate
Helios
Hermes
Hypnos
Ithunn

Njorth
Osiris
Saturn
Selene
Somnus
Trivia
Uranus
Varuna
Vishnu
Vulcan

7 LETTERS
Artemis
Bacchus
Bellona
Bona Dea
Demeter
Hanuman
Heimdal
Jupiter
Krishna
Lakshmi
Mercury
Minerva
Nemesis
Neptune
Penates

Phoebus
Serapis

8 LETTERS
Dionysus
Hyperion
Morpheus
Poseidon
Quirinus
the Hours
Victoria
Zephyrus

9 LETTERS
Aphrodite
Asclepius

10 LETTERS
Apu Punchau
Hephaestus

11 LETTERS
Aesculapius

12 LETTERS
Pallas Athene

Golf Terms

To fill in your holes.

3 LETTERS
ace
bag
cup
cut
lie
par
pin
run
tee
top

4 LETTERS
ball
chip
club
draw
duff
fade
fore
grip
half
heel
hole

hook
iron
loft
pull
putt
thin
trap
wood
yips

5 LETTERS
apron
blade
bogey
carry
divot
drive
eagle
fluff
gimme
green
hosel
links
rough
round

score
shaft
shank
slice
spoon
swing
tiger
wedge

6 LETTERS
bandit
birdie
borrow
bunker
caddie
course
dormie
driver
foozle
hazard
honour
marker
putter
rabbit

sclaff
single
stance
stroke
stymie
waggle

7 LETTERS
air shot
fairway
midiron
scratch
trolley

8 LETTERS
approach
back nine
four-ball

foursome
green fee
half shot
handicap
long iron
medal tee
plus twos
recovery
sand trap
slow play
take-away

9 LETTERS
albatross
backswing
caddie car
clubhouse

downswing
front nine
hole in one
ladies' tee
pitch shot
score card
short iron
sweetspot
threesome

10 LETTERS
stroke play

12 LETTERS
putting green

13 LETTERS
practice swing
rub of the green

Hairstyles

Mullet over.

2 LETTERS
DA

3 LETTERS
bob
bun

4 LETTERS
Afro
crop
perm
pouf
roll

5 LETTERS
plait
wedge

6 LETTERS
marcel
mullet

7 LETTERS
beehive
bunches
buzz cut
chignon
corn row
crew cut
flat top
mohican
pageboy
pigtail
shingle

8 LETTERS
bouffant

Eton crop
ponytail
razor-cut
skinhead

9 LETTERS
duck's arse
pompadour

10 LETTERS
dreadlocks
feather-cut
marcel wave

11 LETTERS
French pleat

13 LETTERS
permanent wave

Heraldry

Noble liege, is this the answer to your quest?

2 LETTERS
or

3 LETTERS
bar
fur

4 LETTERS
base
bend
fess
fret
lion
orle
pale
pall
paly
pean
pile
urdé
vair
vert
yale

5 LETTERS
baton
chief
crest
cross
crown
eagle
fesse
field
flory
fusil
giron
gules
gyron
label
paean
party
rebus
sable
torse
urdée

6 LETTERS
argent
armory
bezant
blazon
byzant
canton
charge
checky
dexter
empale
ermine
falcon
fetial
fillet
fleury
herald
impale
mascle
moline
parted
potent
proper
sejant
shield
voided
volant
wreath
wyvern

7 LETTERS
annulet
armiger

armoury
bandeau
bearing
bezzant
bordure
cadency
chaplet
chevron
compone
compony
coronet
dormant
gardant
garland
gironny
griffon
gyronny
issuant
leopard
lozenge
nombril
passant
purpure
quarter
rampant
roundel
saltire
sejeant
statant
urinant

8 LETTERS
blazonry
couchant
crescent
crosslet
emblazon
guardant
heraldic
mantling
naissant
octofoil
ordinary
sinister
tressure

9 LETTERS
dimidiate
embattled
hatchment
quartered
quarterly
regardant
scutcheon
supporter

10 LETTERS
cinquefoil
Clarenceux
coat armour
coat of arms

cockatrice
cognisance
cognizance
difference
escutcheon
fleur-de-lis
fleur-de-lys
king-of-arms
lambrequin
pursuivant
quartering

11 LETTERS
achievement
canting arms
spread eagle

12 LETTERS
bend sinister
inescutcheon

13 LETTERS
college of arms
matriculation
officer of arms
voided lozenge

14 LETTERS
armes parlantes
Lyon King of Arms
sun in splendour

Herbs, Spices and Seasoning

Shoyu want some sage advice?

4 LETTERS
dill
mace
mint
miso
sage
salt

5 LETTERS
basil
chive
clove
cress
cumin
shoyu
tansy
thyme

6 LETTERS
borage
capers
chilli
fennel
garlic
ginger
nam pla

nutmeg
savory
tamari
wasabi

7 LETTERS
aniseed
bayleaf
canella
chervil
coconut
mustard
oregano
paprika
parsley
saffron

8 LETTERS
allspice
cardamom
cinnamon
galangal
marjoram
rosemary

soy sauce
Szechwan
tarragon
turmeric

9 LETTERS
asafetida
calendula
coriander
fish sauce
galingale
poppy seed
red pepper
rocambole
soya sauce
star anise

10 LETTERS
asafoetida
cassia bark
lemon grass
peppercorn
sesame seed

11 LETTERS
black pepper
caraway seed
coconut milk
curry powder
fines herbes
garam masala

white pepper

13 LETTERS
cayenne pepper
sunflower seed

14 LETTERS
Kaffir lime leaf

15 LETTERS
alligator pepper
five spice powder

18 LETTERS
Sichuan
  peppercorns

Internet Terms

Is it lurking in a web of spam?

3 LETTERS
FTP
hit
ISP
RSS
SEO
URL
VPN

4 LETTERS
blog
eBay
lurk
spam
surf
voip
Wi Fi

5 LETTERS
e-book
Skype
Web 2.0
Yahoo

6 LETTERS
browse
cookie

Google
lurker
online
portal
surfer
upload
webcam
weblog

7 LETTERS
blogger
browser
hotspot
lurking
offline
podcast
surfing
webcast
webmail
webpage
website

8 LETTERS
blogging
bookmark

chatroom
download
home page
spoofing
WebBoard
1337speak

9 LETTERS
broadband
leetspeak
newsgroup
podcaster
webmaster

10 LETTERS
domain name
netiquette
podcasting
web address

12 LETTERS
Generation C
message board
search engine
web directory

Musical Terminology

Pizzicato your answer.

3 LETTERS
bar
key

4 LETTERS
bass
beat
coda
mode
mute
note
poco

5 LETTERS
assai
cycle
dolce
forte
gigue
grave
largo
legno
lento
major
mezzo

minor
molto
piano
pitch
quasi
rondo
scale
sharp
tanto
tardo
tempo
trill
tutti
waltz

6 LETTERS
adagio
atonal
da capo
legato
octave
phrase
presto
rhythm

rubato
treble
un poco
vivace

7 LETTERS
agitato
allegro
amoroso
andante
animato
cadence
cadenza
calando
con brio
furioso
harmony
stretto
tremolo
vibrato

8 LETTERS
doloroso
libretto
notation

register
staccato

9 LETTERS
arabesque
cantabile
glissando
larghetto

leitmotif
pizzicato
polyphony
quadrille

10 LETTERS
pianissimo
pianoforte

11 LETTERS
accelerando

12 LETTERS
counterpoint
key signature

Nuts

Pecan at this list ain't cheating.

3 LETTERS
cob

5 LETTERS
pecan

6 LETTERS
almond
cashew
cobnut
marron
peanut
pignut
walnut

7 LETTERS
filbert
pine nut

8 LETTERS
beech nut
chestnut
earthnut
hazelnut
quandong

9 LETTERS
bauple nut
brazil nut
butternut
chincapin

chinkapin
coco de mer
groundnut
monkey nut
pistachio

10 LETTERS
chinquapin
pine kernel

12 LETTERS
macadamia nut

13 LETTERS
dwarf chestnut
Queensland nut

Rugby Terms

Try having a punt.

3 LETTERS
try

4 LETTERS
back
ball
mark
maul
pack
pass
punt
ruck

5 LETTERS
scrum

6 LETTERS
centre
hooker
tackle
winger

7 LETTERS
back row
flanker
fly half
forward
knock on
line-out
penalty
referee
crossbar

8 LETTERS
drop goal
front row
full back
goalpost
half back

9 LETTERS
garryowen
loose head

scrum half
scrummage
second row
tight head

10 LETTERS
conversion
five-eighth
touch judge
up and under

11 LETTERS
lock forward
outside half
prop forward
wing forward

12 LETTERS
loose forward
stand-off half
three-quarter

Sauces

Shall I shoyu a Russian Dressing?

4 LETTERS
mint
wine

5 LETTERS
apple
bread
brown
cream
curry
fudge
gravy
pesto
salsa
shoyu

6 LETTERS
cheese
coulis
creole
hoisin
mornay
nam pla
tamari
tomato

7 LETTERS
à la king
custard
ketchup
soubise
suprême
Tabasco™
tartare
velouté

8 LETTERS
béchamel
barbecue
chasseur
chow-chow
red pesto
soy sauce

9 LETTERS
Béarnaise
black bean
bolognese
chocolate
cranberry
fish sauce
Worcester

10 LETTERS
bolognaise
Bordelaise
chaudfroid
cumberland
mayonnaise
piccalilli
salad cream
salsa verde

11 LETTERS
hollandaise
horseradish
vinaigrette

12 LETTERS
brandy butter
sweet-and-sour
salad dressing

14 LETTERS
French dressing
Worcestershire

15 LETTERS
Russian dressing

Snooker and Billiards Terms

Why not plant a kiss on Nurse Jenny's stunning frame?

1 LETTER
D

3 LETTERS
147
lag
pot
red
top

4 LETTERS
ball
blue
draw
foul
kick
kiss
pink
rack
rest
side
spot
stun

5 LETTERS
baize
baulk
black

break
brown
carom
chalk
fluke
frame
green
in-off
jenny
massé
nurse
plant
screw
white

6 LETTERS
bridge
cannon
cue tip
double
hazard
miscue
pocket
safety
spider
yellow

7 LETTERS
bouclée
bricole
cue ball
cushion
English
scratch
snooker

8 LETTERS
free ball
half-butt
headrail
spot ball
triangle

9 LETTERS
baulkline
clearance
long jenny
plain ball

10 LETTERS
drop cannon
object ball
short jenny
Whitechapel

Tennis Terms

What the deuce is the answer?

3 LETTERS
ace
let
lob
net
set

4 LETTERS
ball
chip
game
love

5 LETTERS
court
deuce
fault
match
rally
slice
smash

6 LETTERS
racket
return
server
umpire
volley

7 LETTERS
doubles
net cord
racquet
service
singles
topspin

8 LETTERS
backhand
baseline
drop shot
forehand
line call
linesman
love game
receiver
set point
sideline
tie-break
tramline
undercut

9 LETTERS
advantage
baseliner
clay court

foot fault
forecourt
hard court

10 LETTERS
break point
cannonball
centre line
centre mark
grass court
half-volley
lawn tennis
tiebreaker

11 LETTERS
double fault
passing shot
service line

12 LETTERS
approach shot
break of serve
ground stroke
mixed doubles

Terms Used in Association Football

A list to fullback on.

2 LETTERS
FA

3 LETTERS
bar
cap
net
nil
SFA

4 LETTERS
back
FIFA
foul
goal
half
mark
pass
post
save
shot
UEFA
wall
wing

5 LETTERS
cross
derby
dummy

6 LETTERS
goalie
lay off
nutmeg
one-two
onside
square
tackle
winger

7 LETTERS
booking
bye kick
dribble
forward
goal net
kick off
offside
own goal
playoff
red card

referee
striker
sweeper
throw in

8 LETTERS
crossbar
defender
free kick
fullback
full time
goal area
goal kick
goalpost
half time
handball
left back
linesman
long ball
midfield
pass-back
reserves
Route One
spot kick
transfer

9 LETTERS
breakaway
clearance
extra time
finishing
inswinger
non-league
promotion
right back
score draw
target man
touchline

10 LETTERS
ballplayer
ballwinner
centre half
corner kick
goalkeeper
golden goal
injury time
inside left
midfielder
penalty box
relegation
sending-off
silver goal

six-yard box
substitute
yellow card

11 LETTERS
halfway line
offside trap
penalty area
penalty kick
penalty spot
stoppage time

13 LETTERS
centre forward
technical area

Types of Cloud

What's stopping you from seeing the light?

6 LETTERS
cirrus
nimbus

7 LETTERS
cumulus
stratus

11 LETTERS
altocumulus
altostratus
false cirrus

12 LETTERS
cirrocumulus
cirrostratus

cumulonimbus
nimbostratus

13 LETTERS
fractocumulus
fractostratus
stratocumulus

Types of Cross

The crux of the matter.

4 LETTERS
Iona

5 LETTERS
Greek
Latin
Papal

6 LETTERS
Barbée
Celtic
Pattée
Potent
Raguly
Trefly

7 LETTERS
Maltese

8 LETTERS
Cercelée
Globical
Millvine
St Peter's

9 LETTERS
Jerusalem

10 LETTERS
Canterbury
Crux ansata

12 LETTERS
Pattée formée

13 LETTERS
Cross crosslet
Graded Calvary

14 LETTERS
Tau St Anthony's

15 LETTERS
Russian
 Orthodox

17 LETTERS
St Andrew's
 Saltire

Volcanoes

I lava hot answer.

3 LETTERS
Apo

4 LETTERS
Etna
Fuji
Taal

5 LETTERS
Askja
Elgon
Hekla
Kenya
Mayon
Pelée
Teide
Teyde

6 LETTERS
Egmont
Erebus
Katmai
Kazbek
Llaima
Semeru

Tolima

7 LETTERS
El Misti
Huascán
Iliamna
Kilauea
Semeroe
Tambora

8 LETTERS
Antisana
Cameroon
Cotopaxi
Krakatau
Krakatoa
Mauna Kea
Mauna Loa
Vesuvius

9 LETTERS
Corcovado
Haleakala
Helgafell
Huascarán

Paricutín
Soufrière
Stromboli
Suribachi

10 LETTERS
Chimborazo
Lassen Peak
Santa Maria
Tungurahua

11 LETTERS
Erciyas Dagi

12 LETTERS
Citlaltépetl
Ixtaccihuatl
Iztaccihuatl
Popocatépetl

14 LETTERS
Mount St. Helens
Nevado de Colima
Nevado de Toluca
Tristan da Cunha

Water Sports

Take a plunge with one of these.

6 LETTERS
diving
rowing

7 LETTERS
sailing
surfing

8 LETTERS
canoeing
swimming

yachting

9 LETTERS
canoe polo
water polo

10 LETTERS
skin diving

11 LETTERS
aquabobbing

parasailing
water-skiing
windsurfing

12 LETTERS
powerboating

20 LETTERS
synchronized
  swimming

Winds

"The answer my friend…"

4 LETTERS
bise
bora
bura
föhn

5 LETTERS
buran
foehn

6 LETTERS
kamsin
simoom
simoon

7 LETTERS
chinook
kamseen
khamsin
meltemi
mistral
monsoon
pampero
sirocco

8 LETTERS
berg wind
levanter
libeccio

9 LETTERS
harmattan
libecchio
nor'wester

10 LETTERS
Cape doctor
tramontana
tramontane

11 LETTERS
etesian wind

GO GET THEM!

Now you're ready to set out into the world of cryptic crosswords. Remember what you've learned, stay sharper than sharp, strive to the uttermost degree, and you will prevail.

Just before you go here are a few last pieces of advice to pass on.

Firstly, invest in a soft pencil and a high quality rubber. Mistakes happen.

Secondly, choose the crossword that suits you best and stick with it until you are ready to move on. You might have to hunt around a bit before you find it but you'll know it when you answer a clue and your heart skips a beat.

Thirdly, always look to see if there's any easy clues to start off with. Try to spot the definition part of each clue, and possibly underline it. Then look for ones containing anagrams or hidden words, as these are often the easiest to solve.

Fourthly, having solved some easy clues, you will now have letters in the grid which are part of crossing grid

entries, so this should be of help. There are books
available which list words alphabetically backwards,
from Z to A, grouped by word length. So if you are
looking for a word of seven letters ending in –IC,
you just turn to the appropriate section and start
searching.

Finally, regarding anagrams, some solvers prefer to
separate out the consonants from the vowels of the word
or words to be rearranged. When written down like this
the mind can more easily dissociate itself from the word
or words of the anagram itself. Remember too that as a
'solver' you're an anagram of 'lovers' and that's all it's
about really. It's all love.

GLOSSARY

You may not be familiar with all the terms used in this little book, so here are some brief explanations to help you:

Setter	The person who produces the crossword puzzle. (This person used to be known as the 'compiler' but 'setter' is now generally accepted).
Grid	The squared pattern into which solvers must write their answers.
Grid entry	The answer to a clue.
Cross-checking letters	Letters which appear in the squares in the grid which are shared by clues that go across and clues that go down.
Unchecked letters	Letters in the grid which are either in an across clue or a down clue, but are not shared by both.
Light	Another word for 'grid entry'.

Clues   The sets of words that appear with
                   the grid. They are numbered by their
                   respective entries in the grid, and
                   categorized as either across or down
                   according to the direction of the
                   entry.

Definition   The word or words which tell the
                   solver the meaning of the answer to
                   the clue. The definition is usually at
                   the beginning or the end of a clue.

Definition only A puzzle with straightforward answers
                   of a single definition, and no other
                   wordplay, for example 'Male child' for
                   SON. (These puzzles are regarded as
                   the 'quickies').

Wordplay   The main part of the clue which
                   enables the solver to build a word
                   (or words) that provides a satisfactory
                   and unambiguous answer.

Devices   The methods used in the wordplay to
                   help the solver arrive at the solution.

Linking words	The words which help the setter form an intelligible, readable sentence. They are not essential to the wordplay. Examples include 'and', 'in', 'giving', 'seeing' and offering'.
Preamble	An explanation accompanying a crossword in some publications. It indicates any special features or requirements of the puzzle that the solver must know in order to solve it. These are found rarely in daily newspapers.
Surface reading	The intelligible form of words as presented in the clue.
Anagram	A word or phrase with letters which can be rearranged to form another word or phrase.
Anagram indicator	A word or words indicating that the solver has to rearrange some of the letters in the clue to create another word to produce the correct answer.

The Crossword Club

If you are interested in crosswords, you might like to consider joining the Crossword Club. Membership is open to all who enjoy tackling challenging crosswords and who appreciate the finer points of clue-writing and grid construction. The Club's magazine, Crossword, contains two prize puzzles each month. A sample issue and full details are available on request.

The Crossword Club
Coombe Farm
Awbridge
Romsey, Hants.
SO51 0HN
UK

email. bh@thecrosswordclub.co.uk
website address: www.thecrosswordclub.co.uk